QUESTIONS
CHILDREN ASK

with possible answers

Kenneth Payne

McCRIMMONS
Great Wakering, Essex, UK

First published in 2014 in the United Kingdom by
MCCRIMMON PUBLISHING CO. LTD.
10-12 High Street, Great Wakering, Essex, SS3 0EQ
www.mccrimmons.com

ISBN 978-0-85597-762-7

ACKNOWLEDGEMENTS

I wish to register my indebtedness and thanks to many friends who have enthusiastically
helped and advised me in compiling this little book.

Grateful thanks to the following who have helped by sharing with me some of the
questions children have asked, together in some cases, with possible answers, and to
Ruth Green of Our Lady's School, Chesham Bois, who started me off on the whole idea
of the book and also to Max and Frederica Ali, Sandra Brownsey, Michelle Gibbins,
Pauline Gilbert, Theresa Gibson, Rod and Ann Isaacs, Gillian McNaughton and family,
Des and Pat Markham, Tim and Sarah Parsons, Dominique and Anne Pesez, Marcel and
Cecile Peterhans, Clare Richards, Jan Royan, St Thomas Aquinas School, Bletchley, Nicola
Smith, Julie Stewart and Nick Snode and Joan McCrimmon for their careful checking at
proofreading stage.

Illustrations: pages 12, 20, 31, 45 & 49 by Christy Watson / pages 8, 10, 15 (bottom),
18, 22, 27, 28, 30, 36 by The Benedictine Sisters of Turvey Abbey / pages 39-42 by
Gunvor Edwards.
Cover design: Nick Snode
Typeset in Gill Sans, Gill Sans Bold, Gill Sans Light and Noteworthy Bold
Printed and bound by Index Print, Colchester, Essex, UK.

CONTENTS

INTRODUCTION

I hope this little book may encourage both parents and teachers – and I might add grandparents as well – not to be afraid of tackling an answer to what can often be a profound question.

The enquiring minds of children often express unresolved questions asked by adults. Hence this attempt at setting down possible answers will I hope, be of use to parents and teachers.

Parents after all, are the best educators of their children in the knowledge and love of the things of God. Often quite profound questions are raised which are not easy to answer. Some are impossible to answer adequately, in which case, one must be honest and admit that we do not know.

Children often ask questions at the most inconvenient times. A mother is just at the crucial moment in preparing a meal for visitors coming that evening, a father, tired from a day's work, just wants to watch his favourite TV programme, is driving the car on a very busy motorway, or on another occasion, the following dialogue may take place:

"Mummy, I want to know where God is!"

"Now, go and play with your scooter: I can't tell you just now, I'm making a cake for Sunday when Granny is coming."

Little six year old Sarah goes off, but returns a few moments later.

"Mummy, where is God?"

"I told you, I can't answer that now. Go and play and I'll talk about it in a few moments."

The few moments pass, the cake is in the oven and the question has to be faced – Where is God? When can I see him?

This is typical of many situations faced by good Christian parents.

Gary Chapman in one of his books on the five languages of love with regard to children, maintains that the primary love language for the majority of children is quality time. This means giving a child your undivided attention. In an age where there are so many working mothers as well as single mothers, this can be difficult. "Quality time is a parent's gift of presence to a child", writes Chapman. It means being on the child's physical, emotional, intellectual and spiritual level. It is the last two that concern us in this book.

Charles Wesley, the great hymn writer, was one of ten children and his mother used to spend an hour each week, alone with each of her children, helping them, teaching them how to love and answering their questions.

A good time to discuss and answer questions is at bedtime. It may be story-time, prayer-time and question time. For parents it should be a top priority-time. Meal times, at least once a week, can be another opportunity.

The possible answers given here to the children's questions are, with a few exceptions, fairly short, and are mainly aimed at the junior school age, 5 to 11 years. However, an adaptation is necessary according to age and ability. All answers should express the truth, although in certain cases it may only be a partial truth, which can be developed more at a later age. It should be like erecting a building, further bricks can be built in later, but none of the earlier ones should be taken out.

So, always be honest in replying. Some suggested answers may appear to be a little untheological and open to criticism by the more orthodox members of the Church. I make no apology for this. What is important is that the answers are truthful and accessible to children from age 5 years upwards. After all, Jesus who punctuated his teachings with stories, was often unorthodox.

In a few cases I have given more than one possible answer, so that one can choose according to age and background. Adapting some of the answers to the age of the child is, of course, most important.

However, do talk to your children, openly, about God and Jesus, his love for us, the power of prayer, the different things Jesus taught in the Gospels, especially some of the stories he told to illustrate his teaching.

Children ask questions relating to death, and this is often the case when they know of a relative or friend who has died. These are difficult questions to answer because often we adults do not know the answer and if this is the case we must, as already mentioned, always be honest. It would be dangerous to say that Aunt Mary, who died, has just gone to sleep, as this could give rise to a child being afraid to go to sleep at night. For further dealing with this question, see the relevant section in this book.

Don't be afraid of saying "I believe…" This gives space for the child to think about their own response. Never shun a question: say honestly, "I don't know." After all, to many questions we just do not know the answer. One day we will, but for the moment it is rather like looking at the underside of a beautifully patterned carpet. We are unable to see or appreciate the pattern on the other side.

There are, inevitably, a few repetitions in the answers given in order to make them more complete. Furthermore, to lighten the load, as it were, I have also included several adaptations of amusing stories recounted by Hal Roache, the great Irish comedian.

Finally, although I have had parents and teachers in mind in assembling this book, it could also be useful for groups of children to get together to work out their own answers and then compare them with what is given in the text. The prayer at the end of each chapter is linked with the subject of the chapter and may be helpful in concluding a group discussion or for use in a form of night prayer.

So, over to you all, and may the Lord in his great love and mercy help and guide us all in this important vocation.

CHAPTER ONE

Questions relating to God and Heaven

Many of the questions asked by quite young children touch on God and Heaven and the unseen. Because of this, you will find that this is a fairly long chapter and in many ways the most important. In all cases the answers given should be adapted and changed where necessary, to suit the child's age and situation.

1) **Q. How do we know that God exists?**

A. Everything we know has a cause, a designer and this is true of the whole of the vast universe. It is generally accepted that it all began with the 'Big Bang', and this was the beginning of space and time.

The complexity of the universe points to a mind behind it, a mind that designed it. It could not have come about by chance.

Each cell of our bodies is made up of a DNA code. This is a sort of instruction manual for each cell.

Jesus came and told us that through him we can know something about God. "He who sees me, sees the Father (God)." So we have the unique pointer to God in Jesus. Unlike any other great prophet, e.g. Buddha, Confucius, or Mohammed, Jesus made the unique and stupendous claim to be equal to God.

"He who sees me, sees the Father", "I and the Father are one" (See also the answer to the question relating to the Trinity). Either he was mad, or his claim was true; but everything about him pointed to him being completely sane. For example he cured many people who were blind or crippled, revived people from the dead, created food out of nothing, etc.

Imagine you are looking at a really wonderful and beautiful view of snow topped mountains or the seaside, and a woman with her baby in a pushchair comes along. The baby looks towards the beautiful view but then passes on. The mother stops and exclaims to you what a fantastic sight and you agree. We are a little like the baby, we cannot see God or heaven now, but, hopefully, as we grow we'll catch a glimpse of it in moments of great happiness and joy.

2) **Q. Who made God?**

A. Everything we know has a beginning and an end (a game of football, a family meal, the life of your pet dog, etc), but God has always existed, he has no beginning or end.

3) **Q. Where is God and is he real?**

A. God is a pure spirit. God is the mind that created everything that exists.
For example everything we see and touch has a designer – a simple watch to tell the time, or a computer or a part of our body.
So we can say that God is in everything in the sense that he designed everything. He is the thought behind everything. And he showed us something of himself by becoming one of us: Jesus.

4) **Q. How does God know everything about us?**

A. God is 'outside' time and so he knows not only the past but also the future, everything. We can still choose what we are going to do, to play or to work, to go to bed early or to be dishonest. God knows beforehand what we are going to choose. And all the time, whoever we are,  whatever we do or don't do, he loves us.

It is a little like being at the top of a high building and you are looking down at the street below and you see a man crossing the street. A car comes along at great speed and you know that the car is going to hit the man. It is quite certain if the man continues to cross the street. He gets hit. Knowing what would happen beforehand did not cause the accident or force the man to cross the street.

So it is with God.

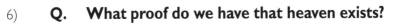

5) **Q. Can we see God in heaven?**

A. Not with eyes like we have now, but in another sort of spiritual way. And when Jesus came on earth, he said, "He who sees me, sees the Father", that is God.

6) **Q. What proof do we have that heaven exists?**

A. Jesus spoke about it, but it's not a place like London or Birmingham. It's a special sort of life where space and time do not exist. It is an expression of perfect joy and happiness. Jesus told us that it is like when we are very happy – he spoke of a wedding feast when people are usually happy. Heaven is when we are so happy we can't even imagine it.

7) **Q. How do you get to heaven?**

A. We are already having a taste of heaven when we love someone unselfishly and are caring and helpful to others.

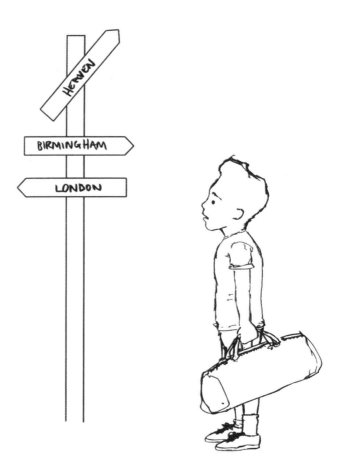

8) **Q. Where is heaven and how big is it?**

A. Heaven is beyond space. It's not a place, but a state, a way of being. It is not up there in the sky. It is here, all around us. It is a different sort of world from that of our earth, the planets, stars and galaxies.
Jesus said that the Kingdom of Heaven is within you. We begin to have some sort of idea when we experience the love and joy of doing good for someone. Think of when you've been very, very, happy: playing a really good game of football, going to the seaside for a holiday, or, as Jesus said, enjoying a great wedding party with lots of friends. On these occasions you don't really notice time going by – a few hours seem like minutes. It's not like a boring maths lesson, which never seems to end!
In heaven time vanishes.

9) **Q. Can you talk in heaven?**

A. Not in the same way as we can now, but we will be able to communicate and share our thoughts.

10) **Q. How can you understand more in heaven if you don't have a brain in the same way as on earth?**

A. We will be able to know and communicate with one another in a different sort of way, which we cannot at the moment understand.

11) **Q. How does God look?**

A. We don't know what God the Father looks like because he's a pure spirit and we can't see him with our eyes as I can see you and you can see me now.

However, Jesus did say, "He who sees me sees the Father", i.e. God the Father. So we can know a lot about Jesus (what he did and said) and so know something about God, the Father, (*see the next answer about the Trinity*).

12) **Q. How can God be three persons?**

A. It is difficult to understand but you can think of water which can be a liquid, a gas (steam), or ice (solid).

In each case it is water. Perhaps it's better to look at ourselves: we think (perhaps of doing something good for someone, like helping Mum), this thought then becomes an action (we actually do the good deed), and finally Mum is pleased and you are pleased and so there is love between you.

This is also seen, three in one, if we think, for example, of painting a picture. Firstly we think of how we are going to paint a lake, trees, a boat on the lake etc, and then secondly, we put the picture that is in our mind onto paper (and whoever sees the picture I've painted, sees the idea I had in my mind. Jesus said, "Whoever sees me, sees the Father"). Finally we and other people look at the picture and like it: There is a link between you and the picture – liking, loving – the Holy Spirit of love. So we can say that we ourselves are a trinity, three in one: thought, action and love. This links up with what the Bible tells us that we are made in the image of God, like God – not with two eyes, arms and legs, but in the way that we think, act and love what we have done.

13) **Q. When you die, your soul goes to heaven. Can you see your Mum or Dad, and how do you know it's them?**

A. Yes, you can know them, but in a different way from now because they will be in a spiritual world and have what we call a glorified body – a little like Jesus after he 'rose from the dead'.

Father John was giving a sermon in church to all the schoolboys.

"Stand up" he said, "All the boys who want to go to heaven".

They all stood up.

He said, "Now stand up all those boys who want to go to hell".

Nobody stood up except little Robert Smith.

The priest said to him, "Robert do you want to go to hell?"

Robert replied, "No Father, I just didn't like to see you standing there by yourself".

14) **Q. Will we ever come back to earth once we are in heaven?**

A. It is unlikely, although we will almost certainly be aware of what is happening on earth, especially events to do with our family and friends. We pray to the saints in heaven, and we can also pray to the people we have known and who have died.

☀ Prayer

O God, we cannot see you,
but we know that you made everything
and that you love each one of us,
and for this we thank you.

CHAPTER TWO

Questions relating to Creation

Many of the answers given will have to be adapted according to the child's knowledge of science, etc.

15) **Q.** **How did something come from nothing?**

A. That was the first thing God did: he made something from nothing and then began the whole of evolution and beginning of life in the universe.

16) **Q.** **Did everything start with the Big Bang?**

A. Yes, God created everything from nothing.
God is outside time and space.
This all began with what today's scientists think was a 'Big Bang'.
When the first chapters of the Bible were written, a long time ago, people thought the world was flat and the sun moved across it, and so they described what God created using the very little scientific knowledge they had.

The theory of evolution tells us that everything that exists, gradually, over millions of years, developed from simple life forms, and changed into what we know today; and we human beings are the most developed and advanced form of life on earth.

17) **Q. Did God make the world in six days?**

A.   This is a story based on the scientific knowledge of the time, and not as we understand it today. The important truth is that the Bible tells us that God made the world – and then we leave the scientists to tell us how.

18) **Q. Are there dinosaurs in heaven – and my dog who died, is he there?**

A.   We don't know, but if they are in heaven, they would be different from what they were here on earth, and they may be in a special place in heaven, where they would be a sort of spiritual dinosaur or dog.

19) **Q. Why aren't dinosaurs mentioned in the Bible?**

A. Dinosaurs are not mentioned in the Bible simply because they didn't exist over the time that the Bible was put together, and the Bible isn't meant to tell us everything. It's not like a science book, it tells us about God's love and the plan he has for us.

20) **Q. Why did God make everything?**

A. God created the world because God is a maker: it's his nature to make, to do, to act. We, you and I, are a little like that. We don't spend all our time doing absolutely nothing. We make things; we do things to help others. And so it is with God. He caused the 'Big Bang' – or however it was that everything began – and he made this wonderful universe and us in particular. He made us to grow and develop in a way to be like himself and, most of all, to learn to love.

21) **Q. How did everything get here?**

A. Scientists tell that it all began with a 'Big Bang', 13 billion years ago. Everything began with this, all time and space, matter and energy. Before the 'Big Bang' there was nothing – only God, a pure Spirit. And God is the designer of everything that comes from the 'Big Bang'. For example, take anything: take your watch or your computer – they each had a designer.

22) **Q. What is a miracle?**

A. It is something that happens that is unusual and does not follow the laws of nature.

For example, if you break your leg, normally it would take some weeks to heal. It would be a miracle if it healed quickly in a few minutes; or, a cancer growth that disappeared overnight.

Miracles sometimes happen in answer to prayer and turning to one of the saints, or going on a pilgrimage to somewhere like Lourdes, where Mary, the Mother of Jesus, appeared to a group of children.

23) **Q. Are there people living on other planets in other solar systems?**

A. We don't know, but it's very likely. However, they could be very different from us. Life may have developed differently from the way we find it here on our planet, Earth.

Perhaps one day we'll have machines that allow us to go and see for ourselves. The thing to remember is that God created everything, everywhere.

24) **Q.** **What are we here for? Is it for some reason?**

A. We are designed by God to be like him; 'to know, love and serve him in this world and to be happy with him in the next' (from the former *Penny Catechism*).

Put another way, it means that we are here to learn to love and do God's work.

 **Prayer**

O God, we thank you for
the wonderful world in which we live
and all that you have made,
and we pray that we may not spoil it
by waste and sin.

CHAPTER THREE

Questions relating to the Bible

A warning to all here! It can be quite difficult distinguishing the difference between the literal meaning of a biblical text and the allegorical sense. Similarly the difference between some of the miraculous happenings recounted in the Old Testament and the miracles of Jesus in the New Testament. Raymond Brown in his books, and especially in '*101 Questions on the Bible*' gives a good clarification of the problem.

25)

Q. Is everything in the Bible true?

A. The Bible (the word bible means 'book') contains all sorts of different books written at different times, some history, poetry, stories, science of the day, etc. It is rather like getting all your different school books and binding them neatly together in one book, so that when you open it you've got to first see whether you're reading history (something that actually happened) or a story (a made up account to tell you something important but which wasn't something that actually happened). Or, again, it might be telling you about the science that people accepted then, for example that the Earth was flat and the Sun moved over it from side to side.

So to answer the question, yes, some of the Bible is true and some of it isn't, in quite the same way as events in your history book, because we don't think of a story or a poem as being literally true. But all of it tells us something about God, who created everything and who loves us. He also has a plan that shows us how to live a good life.

The New Testament tells us that Jesus was God come to live amongst us, and how he got together a group of people to teach us how to love. Some of his followers wrote down what Jesus has said and done.

And this is known as the New Testament, part of the Bible.

The other part of the Bible, the Old Testament, is the story of a group of people who came before Jesus and reminded others of what to do to be good, but they didn't really know that God's teaching was all about love. Many of them thought it meant fear.

26) **Q. After all these years, how can we be sure that the Bible today is the same as the original, and how was it put together in the first place?**

A. There are a number of very ancient manuscripts that go back to the early centuries. Jesus himself did not set anything down in writing, but some of his very earliest followers did, for example John's Gospel was written by an eye-witness. The Church had a great discussion to decide which writings were true and authentic, that is genuine, and they settled on the books we now have. After all, Jesus got together a group of specially chosen men, the Apostles, and gave them authority and power to teach as he had done, and it was their successors who agreed on what was to be included in the Bible (which you might call 'the textbook of the Church').

27) **Q. Are there any miracles today, like the burning bush?**

A. There are many miracles at places like Lourdes; and also sometimes if we pray with faith God answers our prayer miraculously but not always in the way we might expect. Always, in the end, our prayers are answered in the best possible way.

28) **Q. Who were Adam and Eve?**

A. They were names given to the first human beings.
All we really know is that God gave them a soul and they were created good. However, they were tempted to do wrong, to disobey God, and that was the beginning of sin.

☀ Prayer

Jesus, we thank you for all that we know of you and we will try to read about you in the Gospels as often as we can.

CHAPTER FOUR

Questions relating to Jesus

We know a lot about Jesus through the teaching of the Church and in particular the book of the Church, the New Testament.

29) **Q. Is Jesus God?**

A. He told his followers – "I and the Father are one". Yes, he is God showing himself to us and telling us how to live and how to love.

An eight year old girl was asked "Who is your hero, and why?" She wrote that God was her hero, and included phrases like, "Who else would send their son to die for me," and "he is my friend and he looks after me".

30) **Q. How do we know Jesus?**

A. We come to know Jesus and his love for us in every day life, through our parents, at school, at play, and in reading about him in the Gospels and when we are old enough, receiving him in Holy Communion.

31) **Q. If Jesus was really 'King of the Jews', then why do Catholics follow him?**

A. He was labelled that on the cross, because he was the one the Jewish people had been taught to expect – although many of them did not recognise him or accept him. He tried to tell them that he was a king, but of a spiritual kingdom, and not in the sense that Prince William may one day be King of England.

32) **Q. Jesus died on the cross. So how is he alive now?**

A. After he was put to death, he returned, but in what we call a glorified form, different from before, to show us that life goes on beyond space and time.

33) **Q. Looking at the Stations of the Cross, and in particular the twelfth Station, the death of Jesus, one child asked if that was the end of it. Then she answered her own question, and turned to the tabernacle in the Church.**

A. "That can't be the end of it, look! That's it, Jesus is still here with us".

34) **Q. What does it mean when we say in the Creed that Jesus descended into hell?**

A. It means that he went to save all the good people who had died before Jesus came to save us. This 'hell' is not the same as hell, the place for the wicked.

35) **Q. Did Jesus, when he was a boy, do bad things?**

A. No, he did not sin. He was tempted but did not sin because he was God who became one of us.

36) **Q.** **I can Skype my aunt in Australia, talk to her and see her. Why can't I do the same with Jesus?**

A. You need the right sort of Skype – if we pray to Jesus, he replies, but in a different way from the telephone or Skype. And often we have to wait, sometimes for a long time for his answer.

☼ Prayer

Jesus, we thank you that we can know you and love you, and that you have shown us the way to live a simple life to be happy and joyful.

CHAPTER FIVE

Questions relating to evil, suffering and death

There is no clear answer to the problem of evil and the question "Why?" There are only partial answers. Perhaps the nearest we can come to it is in Jesus' parable of the good seed and the bad, the latter being allowed to grow side by side with the good. Then, ultimately, we have Jesus' own suffering and cross, but which gave rise to the greatest event of all, his Resurrection.

37) **Q. Why does God make bad people as well as good ones?**

A. All that God made, including us, is good. However, we have free will, we can choose. Sometimes you may choose to do something bad or fail to do something good, like helping your Mum or Dad, but God still wants you to be good.

38) **Q. Why does God allow evil and bad things to happen?**

A. We have free-will. We can choose to do good or bad things, and God has given us the freedom to choose.

39) **Q. Why, if God is good, does he allow natural disasters and cancer?**

A. Reply of a 9 year old: "If we lived in a perfect world, there would be no room for achievements and learning – in spiritual and physical ways"; and a further reply of a twelve year old: "God sometimes heals by putting his arms around a person, takes away the pain and takes them to heaven".

40) **Q. Why did my young sister have to die?
I'm very angry with God.**

A. It's quite alright to be angry with God, especially if we don't feel that someone we have loved has died. We have to remember that they are in God's presence and when we are close to God, especially when we pray and during the celebration of Mass, then we are very close to them.

41) **Q. Why did Catherine, a young mother die?**

A. We don't know. But we do know that this life here on earth is the beginning of and the preparation for another life close to God in heaven. Sometimes illness and suffering helps to prepare us for this, as it did with Jesus when he suffered and died on the cross.

When Jesus' friend, Lazarus, died Jesus was very sad and he wept. This tells us that God is close to us and understands when someone we love dearly dies.

42) **Q. Will we all die one day?**

A. Yes, everyone has to die one day. Then we'll have a big party with all our family and friends.

The question then continues –

43) **Q. Then where are we all going to sleep?**

A. In the same place that we have the party! Seriously though, we won't have the sort of body that needs to go to sleep.

44) **Q. What happens after death?**

A. Death is a little like taking off your dress or your shirt: you are still the same underneath, but ready to live in a different sort of world, but what that world is really like we can't even imagine.

Father Gerard was preaching a sermon to his congregation. "Every man, woman and child in this parish must one day die", he said.

Little Michael Slade started laughing loudly; the priest turned to him and asked, "Why are you laughing?" The boy replied, "I don't come from this parish at all, Father".

45) **Q. What does the Resurrection mean?**

A. With Jesus, it means that he came back to life again after he was put to death on the cross. However, his body was different from before he was crucified. He had what we call a glorified body. And we, too, will, one day, be like him.

The teacher was asking the class questions about religion. "Do you believe in life after death?"

Little Jamie replied, "Oh yes, I do that".

The teacher responded, "Good, because after you'd gone to your Grandfather's funeral yesterday, he came here to see me".

 Prayer

Jesus, you suffered and died for us,
but because you rose from the dead,
you showed us that good can come from evil
and the bad; and for this we thank you.

CHAPTER SIX

Questions relating to Prayer, the Church, and Worship

Included here is an important dialogue regarding Holy Communion, as I think it is one of the most difficult topics to speak about to children – and, indeed, to adults as well. It is God's wonderful way of showing his love for us, coming very close to us, like giving us a great hug.

46) **Q. Why pray?**

A. If we love someone, or someone loves us, as God does, we should feel we want to tell them that we love them, too, and want to thank them and ask them to take care of other people we care for. God is a very close friend for us with whom we can share our thoughts and feelings.

47) **Q. Why doesn't God always answer my prayer?**

A. He does, but not always in the way we would expect or hope for. He always answers in the best possible way, although we may not realise that it is so.

48) **Q. How can God hear all our prayers at the same time?**

A. God can be aware of all our prayers because he is everywhere. He is not like a wonderful telephone operator sitting in an office. He is not limited as we are.

49) **Q. Why doesn't God talk to us anymore?**

A. He does!

He speaks to us when we read the words or listen to the words of Jesus in the Gospels. And sometimes he gives us good thoughts when we pray, or when a parent or teacher tells us to behave in a certain way. These are all ways in which God speaks to us.

50) **Q. Why do we have to go to Confession?**

A. If we are naughty and do things we shouldn't do, or more likely don't do the good things we could do to help Mum or Dad or our teacher, then we should be sorry.
In Confession we tell God we're sorry and the priest on behalf of God and other people tells us we are forgiven. And this is because Jesus told the Apostles, those he'd specially chosen, to go into the world, to baptise and forgive sin. In Confession the priest will tell us to pray in a particular way or do a good deed and this is called a penance.

51) **Q.   How do priests go to Confession?**

A.   The Pope, Bishops and priests all go to Confession to any priest of their own choice, usually 'face to face' instead of in a Confessional box.

52) **Q.   Why should we go to Church every week?**

A.   Because it's important that we meet Jesus, and come close to him, not just once or occasionally, but as often as we can. Usually this is Saturday evening or Sunday, the day that Jesus rose from the dead. Jesus loves each one of us so much, even much more than our parents do and just as they like to be close to us, and we like to be close to them, so Jesus wants to be close to us in this very special and wonderful way.

When we receive him in Holy Communion, it's like Jesus giving us a great big hug and saying, "I love you Mary". "I love you John."

53) **Q.** **Why do we go to church and others don't?**

A. It's a little like asking, "Why do we play football and others don't?" The church is like a club – a football club if you like, and some folk just don't play  football, while others do; and you've been brought up to belong to the club – the church – and join with others who also belong, through Baptism. However, it's more important than belonging to a football club. Belonging to the Church means that we believe in God and are trying to follow the way of Jesus.

54) **Q.** **Why can't girls be priests?**

A. Boys and girls are different, and each has different things to do as a member of the church and following Jesus. We see in the Gospels that Jesus chose, men, (Peter, James, John and others) to be 'Apostles' and he chose women (Mary, his mother, Mary Magdalene, and others) down through time to spread the good news in other ways. Until now, the church allows only men to be ordained as priests, but there are many who think otherwise.

55) **Q.   Why does the priest get dressed up in church?**

A.   He is doing something very special. When you are going to do something special like going to a birthday party, you sometimes put on special clothes, but beware of confusing it in the way that a 3 year old grandson did. He saw a photo of Pope John Paul II dressed up in all his regalia and asked his grandmother, "Is that an alien, Grandma?" She's now wondering whether he thinks all aliens "Work for Jesus"!

56) **Q.   Why do we have to sing in Church?**

A.   We don't have to, but often when we are happy, people feel like singing; and at Mass we should want to show God that we are happy and want to thank and praise him.

57) **Q.   Why do Priests wear white, like albs, at Mass?**

A.   Priests make use of different colours when they celebrate the Mass. White is a sign of joy and celebration.

Red reminds us of martyrdom – those who have given their lives for Jesus. It is also a reminder of the Holy Spirit, the fire of God's love.

Purple is a sign of penance and death.

Green, like the green of traffic lights, indicates hope and that we can move forward.

58) **Q. In the Mass, how can it really be Jesus' Body and Blood? How does it change? I can't see Jesus there.**

A. We cannot see him, but there are lots of things we don't see but which exist. We do not see an electric current, but we see the effects of it in the electric light.

So it is with Jesus who rose from the dead. We do not see him with our eyes, but because he told us he would be present in this special and wonderful way, we believe what he said.

59) **Q. A seven year old First Communicant was told by the priest that as Jesus was coming to them next week it would be like a wonderful party. His comment on the day was: "Well I thought it was going to be a party. But always at Mass everyone just looks miserable. Why is that?"**

A. Well, really we should look joyful and happy, but often we are serious and thinking when we pray and we may appear to be miserable, although, hopefully we are not, inside ourselves.

60) **Q. Is it really Jesus present in the host, in the bread and wine, is it Him?**

A. The following dialogue is an adapted version of a dialogue taken from an article by Father Henri Boulad, SJ, from a conference in Geneva in 2001.

The priest holds up a photo of Brian's father.

Priest: 'Whose photo is this?'

Brian: 'It's a photo of Daddy.'

Priest: 'Does Daddy travel often?'

Brian: 'Yes,'

Priest: 'Before leaving for Paris, Daddy leaves this photo for you and says to you: "every time you see this photo, you will know that I am with you"?'

Brian: 'Yes,'

Priest: 'Are you going to kiss the photo each morning?'

Brian: 'Yes,'

Priest: 'And each evening?'

Brian: 'Yes,'

Priest: 'But what you're kissing is a piece of paper,'

Brian: 'No, it's Daddy.'

Priest: 'But no, it's coloured paper,'

Brian: 'No, it's Daddy!'

Priest: 'You see, Jesus left on a journey. But before leaving he asked himself how to make us understand that he would remain with us until the end of time. As there were no photos at that time, no canvases, no videos or computers, he said: "I'm going to take some bread." He took it and said, "this is my body, this is my blood, and it's me!" '
'You understand?'

Brian: 'Yes, I understand,'

Priest: 'He added: "every time you do this I will be with you, every day," '

Brian: 'Ah yes!'

Priest: 'What is it you see?'

Brian: 'It's bread,'

Priest: 'Is it bread? No, it's Jesus. What you kiss, is it paper? No, it's Daddy. But that's not all. There is more. Jesus is not like Daddy, he is God. Daddy is a man. But God has said: "not only will it be as if I am with you" – because this photo is not Daddy in his flesh and bones, it's Daddy who is in Paris – but Jesus has said: "I'm going to do more". He is God, he is capable of it. He has said: "It will be me, me truly present." You see bread, but you know that beyond this bread, it is he who is there and that is why we genuflect, go down on one knee, in reverence, because it really is Jesus. It still looks like bread, but in a wonderful way we know that it is different: it is Jesus."

'The Eucharist is the continuation of the Incarnation, God has become Man. God with us, Emmanuel, until the end of time – Jesus said, "Do this until I come." '

61) **Q. What is Adoration of the Eucharist? It is sometimes announced in our parish bulletin.**

A. It's spending time with Jesus, present – the Host, the specially blessed and consecrated bread, and knowing that he is our Lord and shows us the way to follow him.

 **Prayer**

Jesus, through your Holy Spirit of love,
which we have received at our Baptism,
you help us to turn to you in prayer and in trust.
May we always remember to give you time each day
in prayer and to join with others
at Mass each week.

CHAPTER SEVEN

Miscellaneous questions

The purpose of this book is limited to religious topics. However I have included in this chapter several extra questions, including one very obvious question regarding sex because it is so closely connected with religious education, which itself is education in love. It has been rightly said that sex education is "often too late, too little and too biological". Ideally it should be given by parents.

62) **Q. Is there a meaning to life?**

A. Most things have a purpose. For example, a pen is to write with, and our purpose, as human beings, is to love and to show what loving is. It shows most of all in how we treat other people, and how we love God.

Love is like the wind: we can't actually see it, but we can see its effects. And God wants each one of us to help in building up his Kingdom of Love. We do this by being kind and obedient and helpful to one another.

63) **Q. How long is eternity?**

A. Eternity is not time going on and on and on. That would be boring. Eternity is when time stops and we are very happy, as when playing a good football match or watching a good film or with a friend and those we love. We don't notice the passing of time.

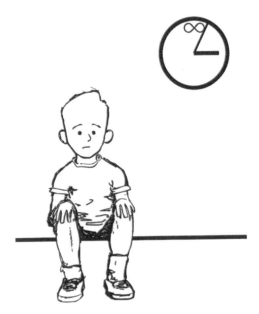

64) **Q. Are there really angels?**

A. Yes. Jesus spoke about them. They are purely spiritual beings, not like us, and they have appeared in different ways to different people.

65) **Q. What is sin?**

A. It is a turning away from God. One way of answering this question is to do what one teacher did.

She put a lighted candle on the floor in the centre of the group and asked the children to look at it, and keeping their eyes on the flame all the time, to turn very slowly until they could no longer see the flame, not even out of the corner of their eyes. They all stopped when they had turned a half circle and could no longer see it, but then one girl noticed the reflection of the flame in the glass door that led out of the classroom.

"Oh, look", she said, "Sometimes you could think you were looking at Jesus but it isn't him at all and you would be following the wrong way".

Richard: "Please Miss, Fr Murphy says that we are made of dust and unto dust we shall return"

Teacher: "That's right"

Richard: "Well he'd better look under my bed at home, cos there's someone there either coming or going!"

66) **Q. Where do babies come from?**

A. One six year old boy asked his father "Where did I come from?" "A stork", replied the father.
"And you, Dad? "A stork", replied his father,
"And Grandma?", "A stork."
The boy then proceeded to do his homework and wrote down: "There have been no natural births in our family for three generations".

It is unlikely that any child would today be told that he or she came down with a stork; although this would have been the case some years ago.

How, then is this question to be tackled?
Again it should involve a progressive education, something on the following lines:

Mum and Dad love each other, and because of this they sometimes give each other a very special hug, and a tiny egg from Mum and a tiny seed from Dad, join together and become a very very tiny baby – which then begins to grow inside Mum, until it is ready to come out and be born.

Later, the next stage could be instruction about how the husband's seed passes into the wife, emphasising how wonderful this is because of their love for each other. And that's why this very special hug should only be between two married people.

One day a mother couldn't do anything to stop her small child from continually sucking his thumb. Finally she said, "If you keep on sucking your thumb, you're going to get fatter and fatter and fatter – and then, one day you'll burst!" The youngster was terrified and stopped. Shortly afterwards he was on a bus and seated on the other side of the gangway was a young lady nearly nine months pregnant. He looked across at her and in a loud voice said, "I know what you've been doing".

67) **Q. How do people become saints?**

A. By showing love to one another, that is being kind and honest and obedient and ready to do God's will. We are all called to be saints by doing the small things well.

68) **Q. Why do holy people have halos?**

A. Years before Jesus came people wore a crown of feathers which linked them with the Sun god, that they believed in. Later on, for good and holy followers of Jesus this was changed to a circle of light, a halo. This later, on stone statues of saints, out of doors, had a practical use of stopping the pigeons making a mess on the statue!

69) **Q. Where is my soul?**

A. It is really the whole of you: the spiritual part of you that makes you unique and different from everyone else.

70) **Q. Why did God choose me to live on earth?**

A. Because you are a wonderful person and he wanted to show his love through you to others.

☀ Prayer

Jesus, we praise you,
Jesus, we thank you,
Jesus, we trust you,
Jesus, we love you.

We are sorry for not always showing your love to others
through not being good and obedient.
We ask you to bless our parents, family and friends,
and those we know who are ill
and to lead us to help others who are in need.

Lord Jesus, friend and brother,
may we know you more clearly,
love you more dearly,
and follow you more nearly,
day by day. Amen

BOOKS BY FR KENNETH PAYNE

Stretch Out Your Hand
(Instruction in the faith for Non-Catholics)

Shades of Welcome
(The importance of openness and welcoming in our lives)

What Shall I Say? (Columbia Press)
(Homily Suggestions for the three year cycle)

Central Line to Eziat
(Thought provoking fiction, including travel and providence)

Thoughts, Anecdotes and Stories from a Priest's Notebook
(Amusing and revelatory)

Joy for All?
(The story of Father Richard Ho Lung, founder of the
Missionaries of the Poor)

The Rosary for Today (www.mccrimmons.com)
(New ways of saying the Rosary)

Love will Overcome
(An enlivening selection from the writings, retreats and
conferences of Fr Henri Boulad, S.J.)

All obtainable from Fr Ken or through Amazon, unless otherwise
stated and proceeds from these books go to help the Missionaries of
the Poor, www.mopsa.org.uk